Keystone Hospitality Development Consulting

How to Open & Operate a

Bed & Breakfast

by

Gerry MacPherson

Keystone HDC

Legal Disclaimer

The information presented here is based on years of experience and does contain some of our own personal feelings and practices. The contents are not the only way to operate a Hospitality Property but we would highly recommend looking at this information as guidelines and food for thought.

We understand you are serious about the operation of your property, this has been proven by your purchase of this book and asks that you honour our efforts by abiding by our copyright guidelines.

Copyright

DOWNLOAD THE AUDIOBOOK FREE!

READ THIS FIRST

Just to say thanks for getting

"How to Open & Operate a Bed & Breakfast",

I would like to give you

the Audiobook version 100%

FREE!

TO DOWNLOAD GO TO:

http://keystonehospitalitydevelopment.com/How-to-Open-&-Operate-a-Bed-&-Breakfast-Audiobook.zip

The Keystone HDC's Solution

When creating this book, it was my hope that it would be beneficial to those of you who will take advantage, but we also knew, we could only scratch the surface.

With this in mind, we are pleased to introduce the

Hospitality Property School Group

This group is designed to be beneficial to hospitality properties of all sizes and categories.

- Within the group, you can ask questions, share best practices, promote your property etc.
- Every month a video will be posted with updates & answers to questions
- Every month, 1 or 2 new training tutorials will be added to the group
- They will be categorised as follows:
    - *Organizational Structure*
    - *Employee Development*
    - *Marketing for Your Hospitality Properties (This will including using social media)*
    - *How to Look at your Hospitality Property as a Guest*

- We will share monthly interviews with hospitality property specialists on such topics as:

Customer Service | Property Management System | Guest Service |
Website Design | Marketing | Employees

- You will also have easy access to all the Hospitality Property School Video Podcasts

  You can watch the tutorials, listen to the podcasts & interviews when it fits into your schedule.

This will be your group, so we want you to benefit to the fullest.

We would like to invite you to experience it…

For *ONLY* $1

Visit the link below for more information

http://keystonehospitalitydevelopment.com/How-to-Open-&-Operate-a-Bed-&-Breakfast-Audiobook.zip

Table of Contents

How to Open & Operate a Bed & Breakfast

Introduction

How do I open a bed & breakfast?

This is a question I am often asked and probably the reason you bought this book. Before I answer, let me begin by asking you a couple of questions.

> ➢ *Does the idea of being your own boss sound appealing to you?*
> ➢ *Is the thought of sharing your corner of the world with guests intriguing?*

> *Have you ever thought about owning your own bed and breakfast, but are not sure where to start?*

If you have answered YES to any of these questions, this book is for you.

It is designed to get you started if you have dreams of becoming a successful bed and breakfast proprietor.

Now, before we start, let me tell you a little bit about ourselves.

Who Are We

We are Keystone Hospitality Development Consulting, a group of travel experts that have come together with decades of hospitality property *(bed and breakfasts, inns, resorts and hotels)* visitation experience.

We have spent 1000's of nights in properties of all sizes and classes worldwide, conducting countless site inspections for a number of world-class tour and travel companies, as well as received feedback from 100,000's of customers.

This knowledge has given us a unique insight into the wants, needs and requirements of individual and group travellers, as well as management and employees.

We understand what it takes to make a hospitality property successful as well as practices that can ensure failure.

This book is designed to get you started on the right track and if followed, when you open the doors to your bed and breakfast, you will be well on your way to becoming successful.

Where to Start?

For the sake of this book, I'm going to assume you're starting from scratch, that the idea of owning your own bed and breakfast is a new concept.

Let's go through a step by step process

Sleep around

Visit other hospitality properties in the area you're considering to open.

Talk with the owners and find out their pros and cons.

Don't be rushed to find the right location

If you're dealing with the real estate agent, find one that's willing to take the time to find you the best deal. If you feel you're being pressured by them, my first instinct is to always walk away.

Study the surroundings

I was once chatting with a gentleman who wanted to buy a bed and breakfast, sitting on a cliff overlooking the Atlantic Ocean.

The building was in great shape, beautiful view and had a loyal clientele and was selling for a very low price.

He wanted to know my opinion, so, I asked him what the rate of the cliff erosion was. He had no idea and admitted, he never took it into consideration.

Upon further checking, we found that the cliff was eroding at an average of three meters a year and at that rate, he would have to move his bed and breakfast within 10 years.

This was a cost he had not considered and passed on the deal.

Examples of how elements could affect a site

- *Is the area prone to flooding?*
- *Where the winds come from?*

Other considerations could be an industry in the area

- *Heavy traffic or livestock farms nearby*

You have to be aware of the noise and potential smell.

Before committing to a site, visit it a number of different days and times so you'll totally understand what your guests will experience.

Make sure your design fits

Building a boutique bed and breakfast in an industrial zone is probably not the best ways to attract your ideal guest.

Is there an infrastructure in place?

- *Do the roads to make your property easily accessible?*

- *Is usable public transportation?*

- *Are there things for your guests to do? Restaurants or attractions.*
  Details like this are extremely important.

Alright, you found the right spot. Before you do any building or renovating you have to decide - who is your target market?

- *Are they going to be vacationers or business travellers?*
- *Young or old?*

- *Wealthy or budget travellers?*

You should have a target market in mind and not try to be everything to everyone.

Now, that you know your target market you are going to have to determine their needs and this can be done by researching other properties targeting your market, trends and technology.

When designing your bed and breakfast, it will be well worth your while to hire an architect or designer who understands the hospitality industry.

Interview them away from your site, their office and ask to see work they've done. When you feel comfortable with your choice, then bring them to your site.

Use the appropriate consultants as necessary;

for example;

interior designers

structural landscapers

electricians etc.

Benefit from their expertise but remember you're in charge. Overseeing this kind of development can be very time consuming and if you're unable to do it yourself, hire someone you trust to manage the project.

Create a budget and stick to it.

Walk and visualize everything

You want to draw out every aspect of your property and even a better option would be to have a three-dimensional model built. You want to understand how all aspects of your property will work together before the first nail is hammered or concrete poured.

I had mentioned you need to have a budget and stick to it but it's also important to be flexible when necessary.

Set a schedule and an end date

Make sure everyone involved agrees to and signs the schedule and completion dates, keeping in mind any outside factors that could influence this time frame.

For example:

holidays, legal requirements

Frequently visit the site to make sure there are no surprises and as each operational area is finished, do walk around, looking at it as your guests would.

When the building renovations are almost complete and you might be thinking…

"I can hardly wait to open the doors and invite the world in, everything is almost done."

Not so fast.

Your property might almost be ready but now you need an organizational strategy in place. In the next chapter, we are going to be looking at setting up your organizational strategy.

Your Organizational Strategy

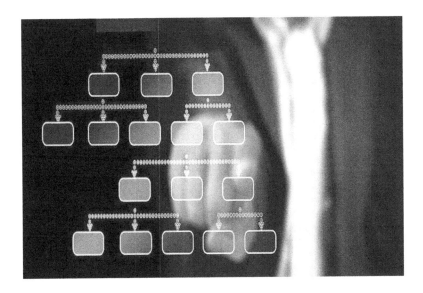

In this chapter, we will be setting up your organizational strategy, but, before we do that there are a few other things that have to be determined.

Why are you a hospitality property owner?

What made you decide you wanted to operate a bed and breakfast?

Which of the following categories are you?

> ➢ *You realize that an early age this is what you wanted to do. You went to school specifically to learn how to operate a bed and breakfast.*

> *You grew up as part of a family-run bed and breakfast operation and want to operate your own the way you saw it ran in the past.*

> *You bought into a business opportunity because it looked interesting or exciting and felt this is something you wanted to try.*

> *You worked hard most of your life in an industry other than hospitality and were looking for a change, a new lifestyle.*

The reason I asked why you wish to become a bed and breakfast owner is that this helps determine where you see yourself in the operation of the facility.

You need to determine what type of owner you would be.

Are you a business opportunist?

- *Someone who has created and owned their own businesses in the past and is always looking for a new experience.*
- *Someone who sees an opportunity in many things and knows they can turn it into an exceptional business.*

- *Someone who loves using their imagination, always looking forward, never living in the past.*

- *Someone who loves to dream and create.*

Are you a supervisor?

- *Someone who thrives on order*

- *Someone whose mantra is "If it's not broke don't fix it"*

- *Someone who has the ability to foresee problems*

- *Does not like change*

Or are you a skilled worker?

- *This skilled worker is the doer; do it yourself if you want it done right.*

- *The skilled worker who is in today.*

- *Multitasking is not in a skilled workers vocabulary, you do one thing at a time and do it right*

- *You feel if you don't do it, it doesn't get done or it doesn't get done right.*

Can you see yourself in any of these categories?

Which of these categories is more valuable when operating a bed and breakfast?

Can you see any problems trying to be all three?

> ➤ *The business opportunist is always looking at new great ideas, dreaming of how things can be.*

> ➤ *The supervisor wants everything done in an orderly fashion, to stay within the system and in the budget.*

> ➤ *The skilled worker in you knows what has to be done, and does not like the idea of the routine being disturbed.*

Today's typical small business owner is only 10 per cent business opportunist, 20 per cent supervisor, and 70 per cent skilled worker; and in most cases, this is out of necessity.

Do you think a better balance would be more advantageous for your business?

If you don't have balance, there are going to be parts of your business that are lacking.

So, what steps do you need to take to become a more balanced bed and breakfast owner?

What are Your Main Goals?

You should get used to the idea that your business will have an important role in your life, your business isn't your life. Therefore, to begin developing a balanced business, you have to answer these questions:

- *What do you personally value most in life?*
- *What kind of life do you want to lead?*

- *What do you want your life to look like when completed?*

- *Who do you wish to be -- deep down?*

great business people, in fact, great people, in general, can see the way they want their lives to develop. Until you can answer these questions and explain to them you cannot really develop your business properly.

The biggest difference between successful and less successful people is that successful people don't wait for things to happen. They work in their lives ... they don't exist in their lives.

**Consider the way you look at things, the way you ask yourself or others
questions, the way you focus on situations around you.**

For example, instead of saying *'why are bad things always happening to me?'* ask yourself and focus on *'How can I turn this situation around quickly and effectively and feel good about it at the same time?*

Instead of repeating to yourself

"Why am I such a loser?"

Ask yourself

"How can I become an incredible, motivating, bed and breakfast owner who LOVES this amazing life?"

You might be thinking, sure I can change the questions, but that's not going to help me change the way I feel inside. OK, you're right, you're going to have to start working on how you feel inside and you can do this by trying the following exercise:

- *write down 20 things you love about yourself*

- *20 things you're grateful for*

Keep the list nearby and refer to it whenever things get tough. You should also keep answers to your main goals with the two lists. Doing these exercises and referring to them every day will help you keep your focus.

Be accountable

As U.S. President Harry S. Truman said:

"The buck stops here".

A central belief of most personal development philosophies is that in order to have a wonderful life one must take complete responsibility for it and everything that happens.

As the owner of a bed and breakfast, you and you alone will manifest any problems or uncomfortable situations that have occurred.

Passing blame to or not being supportive of your employees, can develop a disease that can destroy your business and have a negative influence on your life. Your problems won't go away until you take responsibility for them.

Alright, you might be thinking...

"This stuff is a little heavy, I just want to know how to set up an organizational strategy"

The reason for these exercises is that so when you have an organizational strategy in place and have it actually work, you have to have the right mindset. You have to be able to look at the big picture.

Your goal, in setting up an organizational strategy is to develop a business that you could someday sell or turnover to someone and the operation would continue to operate without missing a beat. You want to develop an operations manual. You don't have to sell but with this thought process in mind, it will be easier to stay focused.

Now, I understand every bed and breakfast owner could be a little different but this is a model that if you follow, will work.

Look at other properties, talk to your friends, research the internet and write down every responsibility you can think of for your bed and breakfast.

I recommend that you take some quiet time, away from all the action.

Don't plan on racing through this exercise, it's going to take time.

When you feel this is complete, assigned headings to the responsibilities. I don't mean individual names but instead titles. When doing this exercise you have to think of yourself as a corporation, not an owner of a bed and breakfast.

Remember, *BIG PICTURE!*

Here's how you start.

Decide what job functions you would need in your corporation?

You need a:

> *President or CEO (chief executive officer):* This person where the buck stops. This person is responsible for the overall achievement of the property; all the managers' answer to this person and this person is responsible to the investors or shareholders.

> *Human Resources Manager:* is responsible for recruiting and hiring the appropriate people to the appropriate positions. But it doesn't stop there. They maximize employee performance by ensuring each employee is properly trained

and fully aware of the employer's strategic objectives; development of performance appraisal, and rewarding (e.g., managing pay and benefits); the balancing of organizational practices with any governmental laws.

Marketing Manager: you don't have a business if you don't have people staying with you. The marketing manager is responsible for finding new guests and retaining past guests. This is done by finding and promoting new ways to target the preferred customer and then providing these customers with an excellent experience at a competitive cost.

Operations Manager: This person is responsible for keeping guests by providing to them what is promised by the marketing department, and for discovering new ways to make the operation more efficient and so as to provide guests better service.

Finance Manager: This person is responsible for both the marketing and operations departments' budgets, ensuring the property is profitable and by securing funds when needed at the best rates available.

Salesperson: depending on the size of your operation, this is a person whose sole responsibility is in the marketing department or could be part of the responsibility of other employees.

For example, front desk or reservations.

This is the same as on *advertising or research person.* Full-time position or an additional responsibility in another position.

Housekeeping Manager

Front Desk Manager

Maintenance Manager

Housekeepers

Lawn Maintenance

Wait Staff, Bartenders
                              and on and on.

If you have a small operation, the sounds insane, but in many cases, one or more of these responsibilities could fall to one person. The important thing to remember is that each of these responsibilities has to be treated as a separate entity and by this I mean each of these responsibilities has to have their own duties, methods to do each duty effectively, and checklists to ensure they are done correctly.

As I mentioned earlier the *President* is responsible to the investors and shareholders.

When looking at the big picture, you have to see the investors or shareholders as outside the day-to-day operation. Their main concern is that they are making a profit.

So, now that you decided which departments that are necessary to run your operation and you have assigned the appropriate names (you might see your name there quite often).

Now take the time, and I can't stress this enough, take the time to determine all the duties that fall under each department and how they are done. When I say how they get done, look at the most effective way and what tools are necessary to complete each task.

Document this in the simplest form, and I don't need to sound disparaging here but they should be written so that a child could understand.

Talk your colleagues, brainstorm, and come up with easy-to-understand methods to complete each task that will, in turn, save you time and money.

When this is done for every duty that is necessary to operate your property, you will have an operations manual that can be used for training and guidelines for you and your employees.

Once the operations manual is completed to your satisfaction you will see a vast improvement in the consistency of your operations, which will ensure better customer service, employee happiness and increased profits.

I hope this chapter has your thought juices flowing, that you're going to start working on your goals and the ways to focus so you will be ready when your organizational strategy is in place.

Your Management Strategy

In the last chapter, we looked at who you were and what job descriptions were needed to operate your bed and breakfast. We also talked about assigning the right people for each job, determine the specific tasks for each job and what is required to complete each task. This was to be done in an easy to follow, step-by-step checklist form.

When all the checklists are completed and compiled you have a working *"Operations Manual"*.

I would like to dive into the actual operations manual itself, what is it going to look like, and how is going to be used.

When opening up your completed operations manual, you should have nothing but a series of checklists and the checklists should be easy to find.

To do this you divide your checklists into categories and each category assigned a colour.

For example,

- *Housekeeping-blue*

- *Customer service-red*

- *Breakfasts-green*

- *Accounting-yellow*

- *Maintenance- orange*

- *And on, and on, you get the idea*

Each checklist details the specific steps each housekeeper, front-desk agent, maintenance person, accountant etc, must take to do their job.

The checklists have to be specific, with step-by-step instructions on what to do and in what order.

Let's take a look at housekeeping. When a housekeeper opens a door, they do not always know what they will find. The last guest might have been extremely tidy and the room looks as good as it did when they arrived or the room could be turned upside down.

My main instinct with the first room would be to start with the bathroom.

My instinct with the second room would be to grumble and then start with the bedclothes.

What's the difference between these two scenarios?

I wasn't consistent and when you're not consistent, you miss things.

Today, when I open a room door, I would have a checklist in my hand and regardless of what the room looked like I would start on my immediate left.

- *I would check the closet to make sure the guest did not forget anything*

- *I would check the lamp to make sure the lights worked and was plugged in*

- *I would look in the dresser drawers to make sure the extra pillows and blankets were there*

I would continue around the room checking off my list as I went to make sure nothing was missed.

My checklist would have a drawing of that particular room on the back of the page and as well as checking off my list, I would check off each area on the drawing as my tasks were completed. I would do the same in the bathroom, kitchenette, at the windows, and under the bed.

My checklist would also have a space for any repairs required and I would fill out a request for maintenance form.

The checklist would cover every detail of that room and when the checklist and drawings were all marked finished, I would feel confident that this room was complete.

I would then sign the bottom of the checklist confirming everything is done.

Now, you might have some on employees who do not like the idea of being monitored like this. I've heard some say they felt like children.

Have you ever gone to the grocery store knowing you had to pick up three items, get to the store and only remember two of the items?

If you have a checklist, that would not be a problem.

If you run into this problem with employees not wanting to change, ask them how they would feel the next time they jump on a flight, they found out the pilot and co-pilot did not do a pre-flight check or the next time their car was in for a safety inspection, the mechanic just looked at it and said *"looks good to me"*, without looking under the hood or when your child was in to see the doctor and the doctor just touched their head and said *"perfectly healthy"* ... you might be a little concerned.

You might say, *"These are very important, of course, they should do more checking"*.

Well, your business is very important and you and your employees, having a good work ethic is very important for your business.

With this step-by-step system in place, you will be ensured your employees will retain consistency and the chance to show real pride in their work.

We have all heard the stories of the person going in for an operation and having the wrong leg amputated or lung removed. This happened because doctors went into the operating room assuming they knew what they're doing. More and more hospitals are incorporating checklists into their day-to-day procedure.

Okay, back to housekeeping.

So, the housekeeper arrives in the morning and checks their mailbox (they should have a mailbox) to find which rooms will be vacated today and to get the appropriate package of checklists to go with each room.

These would be prepared the night before by you or your night auditor.

Each room package would include the room checklist, maintenance or repair requests, and any special requests for incoming guests, as well as any other checklists you feel necessary.

As each room is completed, both the front and back of the checklists are signed, and then this package goes to their immediate supervisor. The supervisor can then do follow-up or spot checks to make sure nothing was missed.

This should not be taken personally, as in even the most organized companies there are times when things are missed. If this does happen on a regular basis, however, there might be grounds for reassignment or dismissal of the employee.

With a system like this in place, even a brand new employee would not require days or even weeks of training and monitoring, instead, they would be turning over rooms like a pro in no time.

Let's look at customer service as another example.

You have a returning customer, and that customer has a file that indicates they had taken advantage of your spa their last visit.

When the customer arrives, your front-desk agent follows a checklist which includes, check customer's likes and dislikes and they know to ask

"Would you like me to book your spa appointment for this afternoon or tomorrow?"

This is before the customer has even mentioned the possibility of a spa appointment. They might not have planned to use the facility, but now given the option might consider taking advantage. This is an excellent example of how a checklist could work for an upsell.

You might ask *"what else should I have a checklist for?"* the simple answer

EVERYTHING!

- *When the outdoor lights turn on*

- *How much fruit should be in the bowl at reception and how it should be arranged*

- *What bills have to be paid and when*

- *What items are recycled*

- *How the towels should be folded*

- *How a uniform should be worn*

You get the idea, everything should have a checklist, with diagrams.

If you have this system in place and work it properly, there will rarely be any errors - **it works!**

In no time, you will be amazed by the number of people to come up to you and thank you for the way they've been treated. In many cases, this consistency happens because of your checklists.

You might be thinking, *"Following the same checklists every day, is going to get boring for me and my employees?"*

I should mention that your *"operation manual"* will be worth its weight in gold but that does not mean its set in stone. It has to be treated like a living, breathing entity.

If your employees are working off their checklists and come to you because there are aspects of it they do not like, you ask them

"Okay, how would you change it?" and if they come up with a way that will improve the service and or save your business money, change it!

And after you change it, reward your employee. This can be done financially, gift certificates or time off, if possible.

The only guideline you should have is that…

> *"Any criticism is constructive and with an alternative option."*

I have seen when employees have been given this type of freedom in the development of their work routine, they have come up with some great ideas and in turn a wonderful a sense of pride.

What Should Your Operation Manual Include?

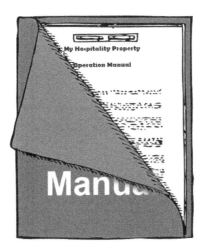

I'm not going to tell you exactly what your operations manual should include because it's up to you. The material could vary a little bit from property to property but the frame or structure I'm going to share with you is universal.

Okay, here we go

It should include the following:

- *Company History, Vision & Organization*

- *Products & Services*
- *Policies*

- *Position Statements*

- *Systems (how it's done)*

Statistically, nine out of every 10 businesses fail within the first five years, this is why you should not look at your bed and breakfast, as an independent business.

If you look at McDonald's, Starbucks, big chain hospitality properties, more of them succeed because they are set up for consistency - they are franchises and 75% or more of franchises succeed.

Part of the reason for their success is due to having a standard operations manual in place.

If you're a small bed and breakfast your chances of success will increase dramatically if you are determined and take the time to develop an operations manual.

As I mentioned before, your operations manual should be treated as a living, breathing entity and can be amended accordingly as trial and error findings are made.

When designing this manual, you must always have in the back your mind,

"Can I open a second location with this operations manual model and not have any problems?"

or

"Can I open 10 locations with this operations manual model and not have any problems?"

or

"Can I open 1000 locations with this operations manual model and not have any problems?"

Your goal must be to develop the best working system of the operations manual model and when it's complete your system must work like clockwork.

So, what should go in your operations manual model?

As I said before

EVERYTHING!

An example I have used in the past is McDonald's.

The next time you walk into one of their locations, take a moment to look at their operation.

- *Look at the décor of the restaurant*

- *How you are greeted by the employee*

- *Their uniforms*

- *The distance between the ovens-to the burger slides-to the register*

- *How the fries are cooked on a timer*

In theory, no matter what location you find yourself in a McDonald's restaurant all the above will be the same. The reason, they are all working from the same operations manual model.

You may or may not enjoy the franchise but there is no way you cannot respect their system.

You might be thinking

"I'm in the bed and breakfast industry, why are you talking about McDonald's?"

That is easy, the theory is the same, it's an operations manual model that works so, there is no reason for you to try and rediscover the wheel, copy a model that works and use it.

Your operations manual will contain a large amount of information including, a detailed organizational role responsibility list (who was responsible for what, with a diagram if applicable)

What else should you include in your operations manual model? Ready?

1) *The location of your site*

   Description:

   - The amount of foot traffic you attract

- The amount of drive-by traffic you attract

- Area and your customers' demographics (age, sex, lifestyle)

- Distance from a population centre

- What is your highway access like?

- The distance to complementary businesses.

Reason:

Your location will tell you a lot about your business. Is your location easily accessible to your target clientele?

2) *Training*

It is imperative that you have this aspect of your operations manual model correct. The training must be step-by-step, and easy to understand by even the lowest possible skill level. You should also be specific on how your training will proceed.

When the employees are hired or change position?

Not so preferable

On a regular basis?

Preferable

Who is responsible for the training and what are the necessary materials needed?

3)   *Your Properties Set-up*

What equipment, furnishings, and accessories are required? Include prices if possible.

4)   *Supplies and Inventory*

For a bed and breakfast, this would include: room supplies, bedding, towels, bathroom accessories, cleaning supplies, vacuum cleaners, marketing materials, if you have a restaurant food inventory etc. You'll also include the quantity, the supplier or suppliers, the price etc.

5)   *Your Staff's Uniforms*

You have to decide how you would like to present to you and your staff to your customers. Professionally dressed or casual? Is the dress consistent and does it have your business name and logo?

6)   *Marketing Efforts*

What is the marketing you use? Who is your target customer? What are the platforms and the percentage of your marketing budget allocated each?

7)   *Personnel*

(a) Responsibilities

An organization chart of the duties and who is responsible. Including who is responsible at every level is very important in this section. Also, include who is to follow-up.

(b) Perfect Employee Profiles

What skills are necessary for each role? The type of personality required? Do they have to be team-oriented?

(c) Job Descriptions

Refer to the organizational chart and be more specific.

(d) How do you find your potential employees?

Where do you recruit, how do you recruit, would you call for referrals?

(e)Interviewing and background checks

A prepared list of interview questions for each position. How to do background and referral checks

(f) Pre-employment testing

The policy and procedure for pre-employment testing.

(g) New Employee Orientation and Training

A new employee orientation and training process. It is very important that this be thorough and consistent.

(h) Communicating and Personnel Policies

Having a proper communication system in place is crucial to the success of your operation.

(i)   Paying Your Employees

When and the system to be used, as well as the procedure for bonuses.

(j)   Scheduling for Employees

How are vacations handled, time off requests, and a plan to make sure all is fair and consistent.

(k) Employee Management Forms

This is for current and new staff to review old and new procedures. Ongoing training.

(l)   Employee Morale / Motivation

Would you like to come to work every day to the same old day and day out routine, nothing ever changes? Neither would your employees. It is important to keep your employees motivated and to have systems in place to accomplish this.

- *Keep track of what factors create good morale*
- *Signs of bad morale*
- *Ways to improve motivation and morale*

(m) Performance Evaluation

When and what is the standard? Are they once a year, twice a year or ongoing? What is the system you use? Do you have a motivation component included in your evaluations?

(n) Employee Discipline

Here it is extremely important to document everything.

Documentation – witnesses - signatures.

> i.   *Resignation*
> ii. *Termination*
> iii. *Post-separation procedures*
> iv. *Final paychecks*
> v. *Explaining termination to other employees*
> vi. *Giving references*

(p) Good Employee Management Practices

What practices and gratitude policy do you have in place for employees and management?

Daily Operating Procedures

1) ***What is your hospitality properties operating procedures***
When will you be open?

2) *Customer Service Procedures*
Here you cannot have too much detail. Great customer service is the lifeblood of your business.

a. Customer Service Viewpoint

> i   *Customer Feedback*
> *How you will judge the effectiveness of your system?*

ii   *Customer Complaints*
A customer complained process

iii   *What is your Customer Complaint Policy?*
This has to be step-by-step.

iv   *Refund Requests (Your policy?)*

b. Service Procedures

This is done to consistently to provide great customer service. For example.

i.   *Greeting customers*

ii.   *Answering the telephone*

iii.   *Atmosphere*

iv.   *Understanding the product offerings*

v.   *Working / interacting with customers*

vi.   *Job descriptions*

vii.   *Suggested selling techniques*

viii.   *Passive selling versus active selling*

c. Do you have merchandise?

Does your merchandise fit with your business's image?

How will it be displayed?

Will there be signage?

d.   Meal Preparation Procedures

Here again, consistency is very important.

  i   *Prepping procedures*

  ii   *Setting up the stations*

  iii *Consistent recipes*
  iv   *Preparation procedures for everything*

  i   *Maintaining inventory*

  ii   *Dishwashing / Sanitation procedures*

e.   Transacting Sales

You don't want your employees figuring this out on the fly as they are ringing up a customer, so they have to know how to:

  i   *Cash Handling Procedures*

  ii   *Accepting Personal Checks (does not really apply anymore)*

  iii *Accepting Credit Cards, Debit Cards*

  iv   *Suggested Prices*

f.   Gift Certificates

  i   *The Issuing of Gift Certificates*

  ii   *Redeeming Gift Certificates*

g. Inventory Management

i *What is the minimum inventory level before ordering?*

ii *Who orders?*

iii *How much is ordered?*

iv *Who is the supplier?*

v *What is the price?*

vi *What are the order procedures?*

vii *How to change suppliers*

viii *Receiving procedures*

ix *Storing procedures*

x *Labelling and inventorying rotation*

xi *What to do with spoilage*

xii *How is waste handled?*

h. Operational and Financial Reporting

You might be surprised to hear that I have met many bed and breakfast owners that are so nervous about their books that they ignore them. Keeping weekly profit and loss income statements have to be at the top of your list as well as tracking the metrics of your business.

i   *Who is responsible?*

ii   *What and when reports should be generated*

iii   *Analyzing the reports*

i.   *Loss Prevention Techniques*

How are you going to audit for theft? What is the policy for documenting and follow through on suspected theft?

i   *Cash*

ii   *Inventory*

j.   Required Cleaning and Maintenance

Dirt in the corners or cobwebs on the ceiling is a major turnoff for me. It has been my experience that customers tend not to return to dirty establishments, especially if you handle food.

So what is your …

i   *Daily Cleaning and Maintenance*

ii   *Weekly Cleaning and Maintenance*

iii   *Monthly Cleaning and Maintenance*

k.   Safety Procedures

Employee time off due to a preventable accident or injury can be very difficult for employee morale and your bottom line. Safety programs can go a long way, an ounce of prevention is worth a pound of cure

 i *Preventing accidents and injuries*

 ii *Crisis management policy*

 iii *Reporting accidents*

 iv *Worker's compensation issues*

 v *Fire safety*

 vi *Robbery / Burglary*

 vii *Unruly customers*

 viii *Using the alarm system*

I. Sales Procedures

How are customers handled from the initial contact i.e. reservations, to after they arrive home?

 i *Introduction*

 ii *The sales process*

   (a) *Identifying the customer's needs*
   (b) *Building rapport*
   (c) *Handling objections*

 iii *Understanding your competition*

 iv *Competitive advantages*

What is your sustainable advantage over your competitors?

What do you consistently do well?

This can be shared with pride.

m.   Marketing

    i   *Promoting your business in your area*

    ii   *Logo specifications (your brand is your businesses soul).*

    iii   *Required marketing budget*

    iv   *What platforms will you use for marketing*

How will you get the message out and what methods will use to gauge the effectiveness of your campaigns? What is your message?

- *Direct Mail*

- *Radio*

- *Television*

- *Billboards*

- *Magazines*

- *Newspapers*

- *Social media*

- *Networking*

- *Word of Mouth / Customer Referrals*

n. Community Involvement

Some of the most successful businesses are those that give back. Your top-line goal should be to serve as many people as possible. Your profit will follow.

    i   *Press Releases*

    ii   *Better Business Bureau /or similar associations*

    iii   *Local Chamber of Commerce / or similar associations*

    iv   *Team Sponsorships*

    v   *Community Service / Charitable Activities*

o. Management Documents

This is an incredibly important aspect of your business – it allows your managers to have a consistent execution of the policy you have instilled and it provides consistent tools across the board.

    i   *Daily Cash Sheet*

    ii   *Absence Policy*

    iii   *Applicant Information Release*

The now after seeing all of this, some of you might be thinking

"Wow, Gerry you're killing me, I only want a small operation."

**The let me remind you of the statistics I shared at the
beginning of this book.**

*"9 out of 10 business fail within the first five years.75% per cent of
businesses using an operations manual model succeed."*

Now, the reasons could include many factors such as your name,
your marketing success and people skills to name a few but the
core of your business will always lie within the operating
procedure.

The operations manual module is the *Keystone* of your business
and to your success.

Like how I did that☺?

How Will I Know My Operations Manual Works?

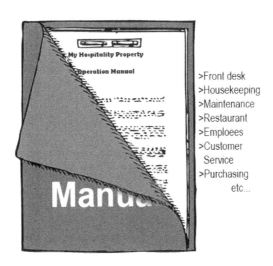

In the last couple of chapters, we have looked at your operations manual.

We were looking at the framework or the structure, and in the last chapter, I gave you examples of the type of forms you would want to be included.

I understand, to some of you, the list might have seemed extreme, but I am serious when I say you have to have documentation for everything.

Okay, you've got your organizational structure in place, everybody knows their responsibilities, their duties and how to perform them step-by-step.

Now, you have to ask yourself *"When it is complete, will it work?"*

To know this you have to ask yourself another question

"Will the concept, my operations manual be saleable?" And then you have to ask *"Will I be able to clone it? And if so will it provide good returns?"*

Yes, I want you to look at your business as a product and this is a product you want to sell.

No, I'm not telling you-you have to go out and sell your bed and breakfast, but for you to know for sure that your operational procedure, your operations manual works, you have to put your head in a different mindset and look at your property as a product.

I want to force you to think that the business system you are creating is a business you're going to sell, and it would work once it was sold no matter who bought it.

I've had many bed and breakfast owners tell me they have no idea how they would do this. It could be difficult for some, and it may sound a little strange for a bed and breakfast owner that they have to start thinking of their property as a systems-dependent business, not a people-dependent business.

Your system, your operations, has to work flawlessly, even without you.

And yes, I've heard.

> *"Work without me, I'm the heart and soul of this business,*
> *it can't work without me."*

Yes, I've heard that more than once.

I know it's tough, but thinking like this will not work if you are actually trying to determine whether your system works.

Don't think of yourself as a boss of a bed and breakfast, but more like an engineer working on a pre-production prototype of a product you want mass-produce.

You want to think of Henry Ford when he was developing his system to mass-produce automobiles, an assembly line system, and a system that could be replicated over and over again.

Okay, you have to focus, you have to think like Henry Ford and Ray Kroc of McDonald's. You have to think of your bed and breakfast as a sample, a model of 10, 100's, of 1000's of bed and breakfasts to come.

At your business, your model will become a place where all your theories are put to test to see how well they work before becoming part of your operations manual and operational in your business.

Every possible detail of your business system will be first tested and scrutinized intensively at your property model.

There will be no detail too trivial, you will have to pay attention to all the little things.

And then what you should soon begin to realize, is that you are now working on your business and not in it.

When you reach that point, you will begin to realize that the purpose of your life is not to serve your business, but instead, the purpose of your business is to serve your life.

Your life and business are two totally separate things.

You will very quickly begin asking yourself questions differently, instead of saying

> *"This is a crazy mess, how am I going to fix it."* You will say *"Our policy for this situation is – this. Is there any way this policy can be improved and if approved, will it work in all situations?"*

You will now be wondering if this clone will replicate perfectly.

> *You are now working the business, business is not working you.*

What considerations will you have to take and a factor when working with your property model?

Your property model has to work with people have the lowest possible skill level.

1. *Your property model will stand out as a place of incredible order.*

2. *Your property model will have a uniform colour (branding), dress and facility code.*

3. *Your property model will provide consistent predictable service to your customers.*

4. *All the work at your property model will be documented in the operations manual.*

5. *Your property model will deliver consistent value to your customers, employees, suppliers and lenders, above and beyond their expectations.*

Now don't get stressed, this is going to be a continuous work in progress with each aspect of your property model going through a natural progression.

- *They will be to innovate the initial thoughts*

- *Measuring the viability and then*

- *Adapting, adding it to the operations manual*

Now you have to set your criteria, your benchmarks.

- When do you wish your property model be completed?

    o In one year?

    o Three?

    o 10 years?

- Who is your clientele?

  o Local?

  o Regional?

  o International?
- Are your clientele

  o Business people?

  o Families?

  o Singles?

- What are your criteria regarding

  o Customer service?

  o Food Service?

  o Cleanliness?

  o Employee training?

And on and on.

If you don't have firm criteria, your standards will be all over the place.

This is going to be a lot of work, but you don't have to do it all at once, it will be ongoing.

To help you through this initial process, I want you to use your imagination.

Imagine, if you will, your property model is working like a charm. Your operations manual has every plausible situation covered.

You come to your business every day and it is full of happy customers and fulfilled   employees.

A gentleman walks through the door with a sack full of money and he tells you he has heard all about your business and would like to have one just like it.

And you say to him *"let me show you how it works"*.

You guide him through your bed and breakfast, showing him how each element of your business works and how it works with every other element.

You introduce him to your employees and when he's asking them all kinds of questions, you feel confident and are able to stand back as they proudly explain how everything works.

You feel comfortable with a thought, you can spend as much time with this buyer as you would like, knowing your business will not be affected.

Imagine, how impressed the potential buyer will be when he sees the cleanliness, order and control.

Imagine how would you feel when he says *"your property looks good now, but what happens if you have to leave?"* and you tell him *"I'm leaving for a month-long cruise the next week, and I don't have a worry in the world"*.

This might sound a little farfetched but I've seen it work over and over and over again.

There is no question in my mind this could be your life, but you have to start by starting.

Start with your criteria, put your organizational structure in place, and determine the tasks that fall under each department along with step-by-step procedures to complete them.

That is how you start.

Slowly, begin developing your property model and build your operations manual.

Will the property model work? *"Yes!"* It does work if worked properly.

It can't be done half-heartedly, it has to be done intelligently, reasonably, intentionally, systematically, and compassionately.

If it is worked in the right spirit, it will work every time it's applied because it requires the full engagement of the people working it.

You will notice, that when you constructively introduce the development of your property model, it will create instant positive change in you and the people around you.

That is the key to its success.

It is important to remember that everybody involved in this process knows the aim and the final goal. When this is done it becomes real and something tangible.

Is your head ready to explode or is some of this starting to make sense?

I encourage you to take the time to read the chapters again, have your pen and paper and write down any notes or thoughts you may have.

What is Outsourcing?

In this chapter we are looking at outsourcing by asking and answer the following questions:

> *What is outsourcing?*

> *Why would I need to outsource?*

> *When to outsource?*

> *What duties could I outsource?*

> *Where do I look to find outsourcing?*

Alright, there is a bit to cover so let's get started.

What is outsourcing?

This is a very simple answer, outsourcing is contracting work outside your place of business.

This could be down the street to the local accounting firm or off-shore to hire a VA (virtual assistant – could be a jack of all trades or detailed to a specific task).

Why would I need to outsource?

Earlier in the book, I talked about the type of operator you might to be; a business opportunist, the supervisor, or a skilled worker. I also said in a perfect world, a balance of all three would be the best. That's not being realistic and I know how difficult that can be.

Setting up a great organizational system will help alleviate many responsibilities that are currently falling on your shoulders but you will find some duties or responsibilities that would be difficult to compete with you or your present staffs' lack of time or expertise.

This is where outsourcing can help.

Big businesses have long seen outsourcing as a strategy, and today's technology has made it a more accessible tool for small businesses, and for many, outsourcing has made a powerful impact on their growth, productivity and bottom line.

Most business owners have great talents, but many times they think they can do it all.

Does this sound familiar?

In reality, you might think or wish you could do it all, but if you step back, you will soon realize that there are other people out there that can not only do it better, but it also does it cheaper than your time is worth, and the result will be far better.

Taking the first steps toward outsourcing can be time-consuming, but figuring out how to build your business with help from outside professionals can offer increased efficiencies and your profits.

By letting go of some of the reins, you will free up more to focus on more important things in your business.

When to Outsource?

When you and your current employees are unable to manage the day-to-day business of your property, it may be time to consider outsourcing.

I would not wait until it was too late. As soon as you see the workload becoming too hectic, but you can't justify hiring new in-house employees, take a look at what duties could be outsourced.

What duties could I outsource?

These days technology has advanced to the point where professionals are able to work from anywhere in the world and with little time, you will be able to find extremely qualified professionals. Before you start, just a word of caution, because you can outsource a task doesn't mean you should.

Before deciding which tasks you can outsource, take a hard look at your business and determine your strengths and values. There might be some things you know like to do and would like to get off your plate, but there might be things important to your core business or for security reasons should not surrender.

Okay, that aside, here are the type of tasks you could outsource.

They fall into three general categories:

➢ *Highly skilled, or executives with expertise.* For example, find a human resources expert who could come in a few times each month to provide consulting advice, employee evaluations, motivational programs, etc. This without paying a full-time salary.

➢ *Highly tedious tasks.* Accounts payable, data entry and shipping inventory are a few examples.

➢ *Expert knowledge.* Examples might include: IT support for your accounting system or your network, social media consultants, web designers.

They are all very important tasks, but you or your staff might not have the expertise.

Here are more examples of commonly outsourced duties.

- Virtual assistants

- Marketing directors

- Graphic designers

- Transcriptionists

- Web designers

- HR consultants

- PR directors

- IT specialists

- Customer support

- Accounting

- Tax preparation

- Manufacturing

- Data entry

- Research & Development

- Legal services

- Creative services

- Healthcare services

- Building maintenance

- Supply and inventory

- Purchasing

- Food and cafeteria services

- Security

- Fleet services

- Video creation
  and the list goes on

Where do I look to find outsourcing?

You want to make sure you find the right outsourcing partner. The first place you should look is in your own backyard, your neighbourhood.

Ask other business owners or your accountant, lawyer, or banker if they can recommend a provider offering the services you need. Using online platforms such as LinkedIn and Twitter make it easy to expand your personal networks and are places to ask for recommendations.

If that does not work for you, other options could include placing ads on work-at-home websites, for example:

Flexjobs - *http://www.flexjobs.com/telecommute/employers*

The Home Worker - *http://the-homeworker.com/*

Upwork - *https://www.upwork.com/*

Work at Home Mom Revolution – *http://workathomemomrevolution.com/*

Rat Race Rebellion - *https://ratracerebellion.com/*

Workersonboard - *http://www.workersonboard.com/*

All Stay at Home - *http://allstayathome.com*

FreelanceMom - *www.freelancemom.com*

What is the next step?

After you've found a provider, your work isn't over yet. Ask for and check their references and then take the time to create a specific contract that outlines exactly what performance is expected.

Explain your expectations and the steps included in the job clearly; never assume that contractors are thinking about what you're thinking. It is very important that the requirements and expectations are laid out in the beginning, and don't assume anything.

Be prepared, there will be a learning curve on the team member's side, so initially, plan to spend more time with them and as your team member gets better, you will have the freedom to focus on more important tasks. Once you have spent time with the new member and they have proven they can do the job, step back, relinquish control, and allow your new team members to do the job you've hired them to do.

If you are going to micromanage your outsourcing, the savings in your time will be gone and the whole point of outsourcing will be lost.

While outsourcing has its great advantages for a small company, it can have challenges.

If you choose to work with offshore providers, language barriers and time zones could be an issue. However, focusing on making your own communications clear can help overcome confusion for those who are not native English speakers. And "time zones create more opportunity than an inconvenience. Assign a task at night, and the next morning, wake to find it complete and waiting for you."

The benefits of outsourcing offer business owners great advantages. It allows you to build a team of skilled professionals without adding the expense of full-time employees, and to avoid getting bogged down with tasks that can be completed without your attention.

It's an inexpensive alternative and a proven strategy for growing a business without letting it take over your life.

When you outsource, you can focus your time, attention and resources on your company's main abilities and spend your time setting new goals and finding ways to achieve them.

In Conclusion

In this book, as a travel authority with decades of bed & breakfast visitation experience, I wanted to share my expertise and knowledge with potential bed & breakfast owners who do not have the benefit of a ready-made organizational structure, branding and marketing that chain properties provide.

I looked at the type of owner you are, how to determine your goals, and how to get started developing a plan to construct your bed and breakfast.

I discussed how to set up an organizational and management strategy for your bed & breakfast.

I shared the method to create your own operations manual and how to design it to guarantee success.

And lastly, I explained how to use and the benefits of outsourcing for your bed & breakfast.

Here at Keystone HDC, it had been our experience that many bed & breakfast owners have taken on the responsibility of operating a bed & breakfast with experience levels ranging from

"I can manage a 5 Star property" to *"Wow, what am I doing here?"*

When creating this book, it was our hope that it would be beneficial to those of you who wish to take advantage, but we also knew, we could only scratch the surface.

So, now you have the information you need to get started, where to go from here?

To Continue Learning!

The Keystone HDC's Solution

We are pleased to introduce the

Hospitality Property School Group

This group is designed to be beneficial to hospitality properties of all
sizes and categories.

- Within the group, you can ask questions, share best practices, promote your property etc.

- Every month a video will be posted with updates & answers to questions

- Every month, 1 or 2 new training tutorials will be added to the group

- They will be categorised as follows:

    - *Organizational Structure*
    - *Employee Development*
    - *Marketing for Your Hospitality Properties (This will including using social media)*
    - *How to Look at Your Hospitality Property as a Guest*

- We will share monthly interviews with hospitality property specialists on such topics as:

  Customer Service | Property Management System | Guest Service | Website Design | Marketing | Employees

- You will also have easy access to all the Hospitality Property School Video Podcasts

  You can watch the tutorials, listen to the podcasts & interviews when it fits into your schedule.

This will be your group, so we want you to benefit to the fullest.

We would like to invite you to experience the…

Hospitality Property School Group

For *ONLY* $1

Visit the link below for more information

http://keystonehospitalitydevelopment.com/ membership-site

About the Author

Gerry MacPherson is a travel authority with decades of hotel, resort, inn and bed & breakfasts visitation experience. He has spent 1000's of nights in properties of all sizes and classes worldwide, conducting countless site inspections for a number of world-class tour and travel companies, as well as received feedback from 100,000's of customers.

This knowledge has given him a unique insight into the wants, needs and requirements of individual and group travellers, as well as management and employees.

Contact info

training@keystonehospitalitydevelopment.com

http://www.keystonehospitalitydevelopment.com

Facebook: *https://www.facebook.com/KeystoneHDC*

Twitter: *https://twitter.com/KeystoneHDC*

Linkedin: *https://www.linkedin.com/company/keystone-hospitality-development*

Publisher

At Keystone Hospitality Development Consulting, we feel that every customer of an Independent Hotel, Inn, Resort or Bed & Breakfast has the right to experience a smoothly operated, friendly, comfortable, safe place to stay; we also feel that the work atmosphere should be a place where staff and management can feel fulfilled and dedicated, with a sense of loyalty.

We offer strategies for, and aid in the development of a hotel, resort, inn and bed & breakfasts own unique brand and goals; as well as increase its patronage and profit while keeping its individual integrity.

http://www.keystonehospitalitydevelopment.com/

Notes:

Notes:

Made in United States
North Haven, CT
15 October 2022

25486743R00049